NO HOME IN THIS LAND

RASAQ MALIK

Published by Akashic Books
©2018 Rasaq Malik

ISBN: 978-1-61775-637-5

Printed in China through Four Colour Print Group, Louisville, Kentucky
First printing

Akashic Books
Brooklyn, New York, USA
Ballydehob, Co. Cork, Ireland
Twitter: @AkashicBooks
Facebook: AkashicBooks
E-mail: info@akashicbooks.com
Website: www.akashicbooks.com

African Poetry Book Fund
Prairie Schooner
University of Nebraska
110 Andrews Hall
Lincoln, Nebraska 68588

TABLE OF CONTENTS

PREFACE
by Nick Makoha

Every culture has its own way of dealing with traumatic experiences. In the age of the Internet and the mobile phone these traumas are often captured as snapshots for the world to share. It is easy from that vantage point to scroll past such an incident and detach our capacity for empathy. This is why we still need the storyteller and the poet to document in a way that is not fleeting. Rasaq Malik in his chapbook, *No Home in This Land,* investigates such a trauma. He wants to know what moves the human heart.

There is a rich vein of new Nigerian poets both on and off the continent that Malik belongs to. His cohorts include: Saddiq Dzukogi, Ijeoma Umebinyuo, Efe Paul Azino, Inua Ellams, Gbenga Adesina, Chekwube O. Danladi, Jumoke Verissimo and Tade Ipadeola. They are crawling out from under the long shadows of Niyi Osundare, Christopher Okigbo, J.P Clark, Chris Abani, Wole Soyinka and Chinua Achebe. This new breed have taken up the charge of speaking to the next generation about the new Nigerian landscape beyond the Biafran War, the oil boom and ethnic divisions.

What do we really know about Boko Haram? Rather than just ask the question, he took himself to North East Nigeria, Borno State to find out. Many of us do not get to see the face of war, or more importantly the face of those effected by it, especially in our own country. Even when we do, it is behind the valence of a TV screen or the rhetoric of a newspaper, where we the reader or observer have control. But in an effort to reconnect us, Malik chose a more hands-on approach. Rather than take a political response, he takes our gaze to that of the domestic.

> There is no home in this country because war is
> the only song we hear whenever people hide
> under their cupboards, in their bathrooms . . .

Malik likes the long line of free verse, as he wants us to focus on the people in the world unfolding before us. The line acts to shift the political context from the personal experience. It is also a way to emphasize the breath that cannot be stoic when presented with such atrocities. The poet is grappling with the scales of life. His hope is one of peace in the home of his natives when he asks "In Another World":

> I want my children to tame grasshoppers
> in the field, to play with their dolls in the living room,
> to inhale the fragrance of flowers waving as wind blows,
> to see the birds measure the sky with their wings.

It is disturbing to think that 2.7 million Nigerians have been made homeless due to this insurgence; some have fled to neighbouring countries. However, a majority have been made homeless in their own country. Malik elects to bear witness for those who are displaced within their own country, his natives who are now internal exiles. People like you and me who never wanted to be victims.

There is no right way to respond to war. But he begins with setting the right tone—a dedication to the Internally Displaced People (IDP) who have made Dalori their new dwelling. Malik explores how the homestead is disrupted by the untimely death of the young, the epidemic of the missing who never return, and the loss of civil liberty. War is then no longer a headline but a way of life consisting of funerals, bomb blasts, and extended mourning that dismantles our daily freedoms. These poems are *reexperiencing* through direct observation because Malik knows, as a Hausa proverb once stated that "even silence speaks."

> Inside my mother's bag
> lies the last letter by my uncle. Abdullah, his wife,
> the widow that stands at our doorstep every morning,

her mind remembering war, remembering the calm
face of her husband, dreading the memory of their
son that wakes up every day to ask about his father.
("Leaving Home")

The poet therefore gives agency to those who can no longer speak, or through grief refuse to. He captures their memories that often intrude as nightmares or flashbacks. The aim is to bring our attention to the pronounced effects of human suffering. These sufferings, as the title of one poem reminds us, happen "Night After Night." Rather than turning away Malik has chosen to honour both the living and the dead. Some we know by name; Liatu Habila, Abu Ali, and others we know by group, the Chibok girls or "villages ravaged by the blasts."

Malik knows that by making their story our story we can move past the spectacle to the stories worth telling. Or as his fellow compatriot professor, Wole Soyinka states:

A war, with its attendant human suffering, must, when that evil is
unavoidable, be made to fragment more than buildings: It must
shatter the foundations of thought and re-create. Only in this
way does every individual share in the cataclysm and understand
the purpose of sacrifice.
(*The Man Died: Prison Notes* by Wole Soyinka)

DEDICATION

For the woman cupping the candlelight that flickers in a room
in Aleppo, for her children who curl their bodies in bed, for the stunned
faces of people recovering from the vast ruins that accompany
a blast in Maiduguri, for those whose hands quiver as they search
for their properties in the ruins of their bombed huts.

For missing bodies, unrecovered bodies, drowned bodies,
mangled bodies, dismembered bodies, bodies buried in a mass grave
after an air attack in Borno.

For the undocumented casualties, for the anonymous corpses
sprouting in the streets of Kaduna, for the unheard voices
of people nursing the wounds of war.

For Syria, for the woman envisaging the epileptic future
of a country, for the forgotten names of dead soldiers.

For Ken Saro-Wiwa, for his body offered as a sacrifice
at the Nigerian gallows.

For the urgent messages scribbled on the walls
of desolate houses, for the hurried feet of fleeing fathers,
for the dense silence that punctuates the incessant lamentations
of the bereaved, for the vague memories of distant things,
for the ghosts of towns ransacked by bokoharams,
for the ashes of moments swept by the gale of time.

For the blood-caressed windows of deserted
houses, for the faint voices of moribund people, for the

children who shriek as the waves of bullets sail across,
for the women who carry the remains of their dead
children on their backs, for those who stand like
a statue as the sky becomes smoke, for the nights
of buried dreams, for the prayers uttered in distress,
for people asking for ways to survive without
drowning, for people learning the difference
between home and exile.

LEAVING HOME

Inside my father's suitcase lives the only picture
of my dead brother, his clothes smeared by dust,
his letter from Kano months before they sent his corpse
to us like mail, like the remains of those who found
no peace in their homelands; people who fell like trees
trapped by a gale, people who died in their sleep,
their hearts laden with fear, their mouths full
of strange languages. Inside my mother's bag
lies the last letter by my uncle. Abdullah, his wife,
the widow that stands at our doorstep every morning,
her mind remembering war, remembering the calm
face of her husband, dreading the memory of their
son that wakes up every day to ask about his father.

In the streets there are orphans who scout for meals
in the bellies of bins, children who search for love
in the sad eyes of people who search for their
relatives beneath debris, people who wait in the cold
to receive the remains of their dead, people who pray
as they remember the losses after every blast,
as they remember the houses that become morgues
after every gunshot. In the streets there are children
who sit on stones as we walk past, mothers who blanket
the corpses of their infants as flies invade the air,
fathers who watch in dismay, shocked by the quickness of death.

On the train we say goodbye to our moribund homeland,
to friends who don't know how to end grief, to friends who search
for what remains of everything that is no longer home.

WE DON'T KNOW WHERE WE BELONG

We do not know where we belong because
home is no longer the tender skin of an infant,
the kohl on the face of a bride, the smooth texture
of a stone beneath a sea, the indelible memories
of a lover's touch, the pristine laughter of a child enveloped
by his mother's arms, the peace we seek as we wake up
every day to hear gunfire in the air, to see ambulances
racing to the scenes of bomb blasts, police cars swarming
the streets like insects lured by the magic of light.

We do not know where we belong because in Borno
everybody knows how to narrate the grim stories of war,
how to describe the head of a man blown by bombs,
how to pick the fragments of broken walls,
how to grieve whenever war disperses people
to refugee camps, how to mourn the young
bashed by rifles, carted as spoils of war;
how to survive the repetitive sound of grenades,
how to outlive the thick fragrance of smoke,
how to pray with tears gathering in our eyes.

There is no home in this country because war is
the only song we hear whenever people hide
under their cupboards, in their bathrooms,
under their beds. There is no home in this
country because whether death comes or not, my
children will still ask me when we will
leave this country, when we will pack
our luggage and say, *thank you,*
city of smoke and bones.

AT DALORI CAMP

After Abubakar Adam Ibrahim's
Losing and Finding Love in the Time of Boko Haram

The women stretch their legs as their malnourished infants
suck disease-infected breasts, as another day begins with
fear lurking in their eyes, as they remember their relatives
at home, their families waiting at the doorsteps every night,
their beloveds searching for them every day, their dreams
dismantled by war, their hope the frail light in the lantern
they carry every night to search for the bodies of the dead.

The women weep as they see their children hold
the dusty photographs of their fathers, as they remember
the soldiers raping them every night, the soldiers
littering their bodies with scars nothing can erase.
They remember the corpses paving the streets,
bodies wrapped and disposed like waste
beside desolate houses. The women wake up
every day to see rooms filled with new refugees,
trucks filled with few relief materials for the displaced.

The women watch their children lie on the mats,
as another night begins with people searching
for the meaning of home in the sadness of a woman washing
the blood-soaked dress of her daughter, in the silence
of a man returning home to meet the dismembered
bodies of his wife and children, in the sorrow of a widow
living with solitude. The women search for the meaning
of home whenever they wake up to see bullet holes on the walls,
whenever the pieces of their beloveds fill the streets,

whenever they receive letters from missing loved ones,
notes from relatives in prisons, flowers from dying parents to their children.

COUNTING HER LOSSES

My mother begins with the night we fled home
amid gunshots, the night we escaped the bokoharams
to hide in an incompleted building in Gamboru,
the mornings of sirens piercing the hearts of people
yelling *help* as fire ravaged their properties.

My mother begins with the night we waited for a bus to ferry us
to the refugee camp, the number of children orphaned by
war, their mothers widowed by the blast, the people abandoned
to carry the agony of homelessness like a cross.

My mother begins with the scarred bodies of women mourning
their dead children, the women carrying the trauma of war
in their hearts, the women bearing the scars of exile
like an emblem, the women tending their wounds in the dark.

My mother begins with the soft bones of infants
crushed to death, the tender bodies of children splintered
by missiles, the bullets on the roofs of houses.

My mother begins with silence as her lips quake, as her
hand traces my dark skin, as her eyes map my eyes,
saying there are words too heavy to tell a child like me.

GRATEFUL

For life after the bombings, for the love that cradles us in spite of the war
that wrecks our land, for joy in the cries of infants in their mother's arms.

Grateful for little things, for my son's dream of building the world,
for people waking up every day to marvel at the birds that fill the sky.

Grateful for friends that visit us, relatives that send letters to us,
people that open their doors for us when war looms in the sky.

Grateful for the rivers that become a confluence, fields that house our
children when they gather to explore childhood moments.

Grateful for answered questions, for the walls that bear the frames
of our pictures, for the windows that usher in air.

Grateful for things that shape us into better beings, things that lift our hands
when we fill the night with cries, things that unchain our passion for bliss.

Grateful for husbands that return home safely to meet their wives and children
waiting for them at doorsteps, for mothers whose children remember.

Grateful for things that survive, for children whose lives become maps
for us to trace, for God's infinite mercy over us.

Grateful for the meals taken at normal hours, for shared compassion,
for songs that soothe our troubled hearts.

Grateful for the ones who kiss our brows and say, *we will be fine*,
for the ones who stretch their hands filled with gifts for us to take home,

for the ones who phone at late hours to ask if we are fine,
for the ones whose names mean the world is a haven.

Grateful for my mother's stable health, for my father's strong bones,
for the assurance of kindness when we need it.

Grateful for those who, in spite of their sad
hearts, offer us every bright thing in the world.

IN THIS VILLAGE WHERE EVERY DAWN
BEGINS WITH A FUNERAL

after Elana Bell

In this village, where a child draws the image
of his dead mother on a cardboard,
where a man covers the pieces of his wife's body
with leaves, where flowers replace bodies
buried in exile, where the muezzin's voice recedes
as gunshots assemble people at the scene, where the dead
long for a mass funeral in order to escape the agony
of being devoured by crows, where a woman translates her grief
by sitting on the tomb of her child, they cook dinner with
bloodstained water. The earth widens beneath feet,
as people trace the footprints of lost beloved
with lanterns and return to their huts to meet the mangled
bodies of their children. Here, broken women seek healing,
and men are burdened with the role of burying
their dead. Here, my grandmother's graveyard decked
with a vase of writhed wreaths, my uncle's farmland is razed
to dust, and my family's house is turned into a hollow during war.
In this village there are unmarked graves, tombstones bearing
the names of ambushed soldiers, blood-draped walls of old houses,
remnants of burnt homesteads, ruins of bombed stores, fallen branches
and dry twigs. The hills house refugees, camps built in the desert,
lands converted to cemeteries. The girls here live with the scars of rape,
the boys are weaned by war, elders stagger as they walk
to where a country becomes a shadow, a memorial ground.
The portraits of the dead are taped to the walls,
with the broken slates of children who will never return home
to enjoy childhood years, to meet the streets glowing

with streetlights, to listen to the radio once again, to bathe in the river,
to climb mango trees, to adorn their necks with catapults,
to dance in the rain and listen to stories at dusk.

GRIEF

My mother waits in the cold all night
as my father's absence becomes a photograph
she caresses whenever she remembers

what it means to lose a beloved to blasts;
what it means to wake up to meet an empty bed;
what it means to attend the burial of a relative;
what it means to pine for someone that will not arrive.

A woman sieves a pile of corpses to discover her husband's body.
A woman shows her children where they should bury her.

My grandfather died with our country's name on his lips,
my grandmother said, *do not bury me in this land when I die.*

I have inherited a house where the cobwebbed frames hanging
on the walls bear the photographs of the dead, where each moment
melts into memories of blighted dreams, moribund hopes.

I trace gun wounds on your forehead, plant a flower to
identify the grave of a lost child, carving a homeland out
of the remains of bodies that spread like leaves in a field.

This is not the country in which I want my children to live;
this is not a home to inhabit; this is not the paradise we pray for.

IN ANOTHER WORLD

In another world I want to be a father without
passing through the eternal insanity of mourning
my children, without experiencing the ritual
of watching my children return home as bodies
folded like a prayer mat, without spending my
nights telling them the stories of a hometown
where natives become aliens searching for
a shelter. I want my children to spread a mat
outside my house and play without the walls
of houses ripped by rifles. I want to watch my children
grow to recite the name of their homeland like Lord's
Prayer, to frolic in the streets without being hunted like
animals in the bush, without being mobbed to death.
In another world I want my children to tame grasshoppers
in the field, to play with their dolls in the living room,
to inhale the fragrance of flowers waving as wind blows,
to see the birds measure the sky with their wings.

HOW WE BECOME HUMAN

On the radio: a country becomes a dirge.
In a room in Kano, a woman prays for her
son as he leaves home for school.
May bombs never meet you on the road.
May the road never thirst for blood today.
In another room there is a woman in
her nightgown, her eyes darkened by
the longing for her son on the battlefield.
This is how we become human: you learn
the art of grief whenever people become rubble;
me in my father's parlour in Ibadan watching the news;
me remembering my aunt's daughter living
in Attagara, the venue of the blast; me remembering
Sarah, her body riddled with bullets; Musa, his eyes
blurred by teargas. On the radio a country becomes
an elegy to be read by those who, like me,
will wake up tomorrow to see their country capsize,
as everything dissolves in war.

ELEGY FOR ABU ALI

Your country will remember you as a young Nigerian man,
a father of a girl who will one day crave to see the tomb
of her father, the breadwinner of a family who will not find
peace in your tragic departure. Your country will remember
you as a veteran soldier mowed by the rapid bokoharam
bombs, as one out of countless soldiers who trudged
the hazy paths of war, who rode on the back of a fickle
hope as they fought for a country, who, at the end,
will deck their tombs with a garland of wilted wreaths.
Your country will remember you as a lone conqueror
of terrorists in Monguno, Mallam Fatori, Gwoza;
who faced the bullets when the war front became
a tomb littered with the flesh of young soldiers.
Your country will remember you as a beneficiary
of manifold consolatory messages from your kinsmen;
from Nigerians who reside on the virtual world;
from those who, unlike you, will wake up again
to see the remnants of bombed things, see bombs
crowding the northern sky, see the victims
of war wheeled to the hospitals, dead soldiers
carried like a trophy, lowered into their graves.
Your wife will remember you as a testament
of grief that continues to ravage her tender
heart. Your country will remember you
as another name in the list of dead patriotic soldiers,
as one of the recent losses, as one of the stories
that will be told someday.

HOW WE SURVIVE

Sometimes we muffle the cries of our children
and lure them to sleep with the promise of buying
them Christmas dresses, toys from the market,
balloons to throw into the air, schoolbags
for them to carry to school. Sometimes we
plead to them never to leave home for distant places,
for fields pregnant with mines, for streets paved
with bullets. Sometimes we lead our children to
empty houses to sleep, to mosques faraway
from towns, to places where we watch them
sleep with ease. Sometimes we hide in the dark
as gunshots raid the serenity of the night,
as gasoline burns the air. Sometimes we tell
beautiful stories of imaginary homelands to our
children, to those whose love for their homelands
is a fragment of a crashed sky. Sometimes we sleep
with the hope of waking up to meet a land where the laughter
of children invokes smiles on the faces of the old ones;
a land where people breathe peace; a land where they
grow and flourish, where nothing saddens them
as they breed and live to love and dream.

HOW TO WORSHIP ALLAH

It is time for solat Ishai,
but my child, afraid of hearing
the sound of blasts, moulds a kiblah out
of the corner of our room. This is how we
worship Allah. This is how we pray without
screaming curses on the heads of those who do not
believe in Allah, without spilling blood on the earth
for the sake of Allah that does not demand
that we decorate the sky with bullets. This is how
we worship our God as Muslims. This is how my
child, afraid of being mobbed in the streets, prays
to Allah in our room, in a town where we stay awake
every night to observe the faces of strangers whose
dream is to dismantle our houses with bombs.
This is how we worship Allah without fear,
how we supplicate to Him without burning
churches, without bombing houses, without
desecrating the holy Qur'an, without leaving
towns and cities as ashes washed away by
the flood of tears. This is how we worship
Allah without converting the earth into a
cemetery, without splattering blood on the walls
of desolate houses, without setting fire to huts
and villages in Borno, in Maiduguri, in Jos, in Kano,
in Kaduna, in places all over the world.

NIGHT AFTER NIGHT
for villages ravaged by blasts

The villagers huddle in a room where
the memories of people displaced by war
are dusty photographs on a table, names
of lost beloveds scrawled on the walls.
The villagers gather to burn candles
and inhale bloodied air emanating from
the bodies of people bombed in the streets
of Gwoza; bodies waiting for coffins in Goshe;
bodies in undisclosed graves. The villagers
mourn their relatives whose names the radio
will not pronounce, the people whose minds
are traumatized by war, their distant friends
who see home as a tragedy, as a dystopia,
as a wall burrowed by bullets. The villagers recite
the names of the children towed to a refugee
camp in Rann, the children becoming almajiris,
lifting bowls for alms in the streets of Kaduna.
Night after night the villagers remember
the charred body of peace rotting in the streets,
the dead replaced with flowers in villages
ransacked by bokoharams, the faint voices
of people groaning beneath the debris.

SOMEDAY I WILL BE NO MORE

This house will become a haven of ghosts,
a recluse for dead things to reincarnate in
the smell of dust that billows in each room;
in the frames of portraits hanging on the walls;
in the silence that remains after the death
of a beloved. Someday I will lie in bed, lifeless,
my body and my dreams ceased
by the hurried hand of a clock. Someday I will
be no more and this house will remain unoccupied,
a heritage left untouched except by the inevitable
presence of dense silence, by the cracks invented
by time, by the rust created by sun. Someday I
will leave and never return to sit on those sofas,
to watch the TV and giggle, to dine on this table,
to sip water from the jug there, to sleep in bed
as dusk arrives, to laugh at stories sweetened
by the lips of Grandpa, to learn from the mystery
that hides in his grey hair. Someday I will become
a coffin decked with bouquets of flowers; a coffin
bearing sand, lowered into the grave; waved at
by mourners who, after the funeral, will continue
to live, as usual.

AFTER MY GRANDMA'S BURIAL

We sit on the benches
outside of our house, our mother
in a dark gown, our father attending
to visitors; we children staring
at the grave of my grandma, our thoughts
too frail to decipher the meaning
of burying a beloved.

There are those, we know, not lucky
enough to have a decent burial;
those who lie in unknown places;
those who find solace in caressing
the photographs of their lost relatives;
those who are murdered in the cold
of war; those who wake up to see
bullet holes on their doors;
those who learn how to pray
as they wilt in the fire of bombs;
those who pass through the dark
as they carry the burden of war.

Tonight in the silence that thickens,
we understand how death happens,
how we become dust, scraps in
the kitchen, fossils for earth to
devour, bones that never rise
no matter the force of rain.

HOME IS

Hadiza is breastfeeding her baby without
racing to her room to check if her husband
is alive as bombs splinter the earth, as the musk
of blood cloaks the air like a blanket
wrapped around the fragile body of a child.
Home is my father opening his arms to
embrace strangers, to welcome them to
our room without scanning their faces
and luggage to know if they are terrorists
or not, to know if they are thieves or smugglers.

Home is Rahaman sleeping in his room without
having to gaze through the window to see children
crippled by war, maimed by a tornado; mangled bodies
waiting to be buried, wounded bodies waiting for
first aid. Home is you bereft of grief, spared of trauma,
absent from refugee camps where bokoharam victims
bear the agony of searching for an identity, for where
they belong, for how to survive.

Home is Hazizah and her daughter walking the streets
without telling her daughter to undress her hijab;
without whispering into her ears to hide when
people ask for her name; without leaving her
to bear the trauma of the world like a birthmark.
Home is the land that knows the texture
of rain, the land that knows the aura of love.

REMEMBERING HOME

My father dictating words to me as my
mother stitched torn clothes on the sofa,
as my sister, Hauwa, fixed her eyes
on the lantern that sat on the table.
My grandmother waking up to water her garden;
my grandfather weaving folktales
under the unflinching gaze of moonlight.

Aisha waiting for her son to arrive from school
as the stereo announced the abduction of the Chibok
girls, as her husband's heart became the origin
of fear, as missiles invaded the sky.

The first bomb blast that woke us to eternal
nightmares, the cries of women searching
for their children in the ashes of burnt buildings;
the second explosion that turned our streets to tombs.

The fright that gripped Fatimah as she visited the scenes
of casualties to identify her uncle, Naomi watching
the news on the TV, Hannatu reading the list of the dead
in a daily newspaper, Saratu backing her daughter
as darkness dimmed her room, as her family became
exiled like others who, till now, have nowhere
to call a homeland.

HOW TO MOURN

Begin with the girls of Chibok:

Ramatu Yaga,

Naomi Yaga,

Rahilla Bitrus,

Mary Ali,

Glory Aji,

Solomi Titus,

Grace Paul,

Liatu Habila,

Debora Peter,

Lugguwa Samuel,

Comfort Bulus,

and many, many, more.

Begin with the girls of a country where bombs swoop
and rip people to pieces, to shards, to bodies waiting for relatives
to identify them in the streets.

Begin with smoke spiralling in the sky, smoke walling the house
where a woman hides her son from insurgents,
where a man lies in bed with a severed arm, in a blood-soaked T-shirt.

Begin with the agony of exile, the forced evacuation from one's homeland,
the hasty feet of people escaping through the borders, the weak pierced by missiles.

Begin with the man leaving his family to fight bokoharam in Baga,
his corpse buried like dirt, his burial bereft of national honour,
bereft of his country's flag swaying in the air.

Begin with people buried underground, people shivering in beds as bullets
rattle their windows, people watching as a boy's breath fades in the smoke.

Begin with people panting as they see military trucks in the streets,
people hiding under their roofs to survive stray bullets in the air.

Begin with the old woman sitting on a stool in a dark room in Bama,
her dead husband's pension held hostage by the government,
her children's graves shadowed by weeds.

Begin with the people who will never attend the *masjid* again for fear of being bombed.

Begin with the women arranging the dolls of their dead children,
the women remembering their beloveds by burning candles every night.

Begin with smoldered houses, blasted streets, prayer mats dripping blood,
the laugher of children mingling with the din of bombs.

Begin with Gaza and people massacred before dawn.

Begin with parents dying as if there is no hope of their children's return,
the parents measuring the depth of their grief.